C. A Fox

Victory through the Name

C. A Fox

Victory through the Name

ISBN/EAN: 9783744756969

Printed in Europe, USA, Canada, Australia, Japan

Cover: Foto ©ninafisch / pixelio.de

More available books at **www.hansebooks.com**

VICTORY THROUGH THE NAME

The Keswick Library

New and Cheap Edition. Monthly 6d. nett

Edited by Rev. Evan H. Hopkins

The Series will consist of the following—

1. *A HOLY LIFE*   Rev. G. H. C. Macgregor
2. *THE SECRET OF HOLINESS*   Rev. F. S. Webster
3. *NEED AND FULNESS*   Dr. Handley Moule
4. *JOHN THE BAPTIST*   Dr. Elder Cumming
5. *I FOLLOW AFTER*   Rev. Preb. Webb-Peploe
6. *HIDDEN, YET POSSESSED*   Rev. Evan H. Hopkins
7. *FROM CALVARY TO PENTECOST*   Rev. F. B. Meyer
8. *THEY MIGHT BE*   Rev. Hubert Brooke
9. *THE LIFE OF FELLOWSHIP*   Rev. E. W. Moore
10. *"REALITY"*   Rev. J. T. Wrenford
11. *LIFTED LOADS*   Miss Lucy Bennett
12. *THE SECRET OF POWER FOR DAILY LIVING*   Rev. W. Houghton
13. *"INSTEAD"*   Miss Nugent
14. *VICTORY THROUGH THE NAME*   Rev. C. A. Fox
15. *THINGS WHICH CANNOT BE SHAKEN.*   Rev. C. G. Moore

Marshall Brothers, Keswick House, Paternoster Row

The Keswick Library

Victory Through The Name

By Rev C A Fox

LONDON MARSHALL
BROTHERS PATERNOSTER
ROW

First Edition
    Oct. 1894
Reprinted
    April 1895
Reprinted
    May 1901
Reprinted
    June 1901
Reprinted
    Nov. 1903

CONTENTS

CAP		PAGE
1	JEHOVAH; OR, THE VICTORY OF THE INVISIBLE PRESENCE	7
2	JEHOVAH-JIREH; OR, THE VICTORY OF DIVINE SELF-SACRIFICE	42
3	JEHOVAH-ROPHI; OR, THE VICTORY OF DIVINE ASSIMILATION	71

VICTORY THROUGH THE NAME

Cap I —— *JEHOVAH; OR THE VICTORY OF THE INVISIBLE PRESENCE*

"*He endured, as seeing Him who was invisible.*"

"*I appeared unto Abraham, unto Isaac, and unto Jacob, by the name of God Almighty, but by My Name, JEHOVAH, was I not known to them.*"—Ex. vi. 3.

"IS God dead?" was the startling exclamation of a stalwart coloured woman, as she sprang to her feet in the midst of a mass-meeting of downtrodden, hopeless slaves. "Downtrodden, hopeless slaves"—such is an exact description of the condition of Israel at this juncture of their history, as brought before us in the book of Exodus. And just such is the startling truth God intended now to emphasize in the ears of His people at this very juncture, by the revelation of His great and mysterious Name, Jehovah. It was as though He would say to them, True, slavery, despair, and death are staring you in the face, yet God lives! I Am unchangeably that I Am; and I Am is here!

> "Jesus lives! no longer now
>   Can thy terrors, Death, appal us;
> Jesus lives! by this we know
>   Thou, O grave, canst not enthral us.
>   Alleluia!
>
> Jesus lives! our hearts know well
>   Nought from us His love can sever.
> Life, nor death, nor powers of hell
>   Tear us from His keeping ever.
>   Alleluia!"

It has been said that the proper study of mankind is man; surely we may venture to Christianize Pope's famous line, and say, "The proper study of mankind is God."

God has at various times given Himself a name, or revealed Himself under some particular title. In the Old Testament it was this mysterious name, Jehovah, which on various subsequent occasions received certain qualifying additions. In the Gospels it was the ever-blessed name of Jesus. In the Acts of the Apostles, and afterwards in the Epistles, we meet the fuller name, Jesus Christ, or the Lord Jesus Christ, or the Lord Jesus. In the book of Revelation one name stands out increasingly prominent, as though it were to demand special attention, and would need special emphasis in the closing times of this dispensation, viz., "The Lamb that was slain." Each of these great Names has a history attached to it; each of them is a volume in itself; each gathers up into itself certain aspects or attributes of God, which transcend human speech and knowledge.

God's names are intended to be universal symbols, watchwords for Eternity; names by which we may at once bring God down within the range of human vision, and within the reach of human need. They are concise moral revelations of the nature and character of God, made available and portable for our earthly pilgrimage. It is natural that the first great Name, Jehovah, should be in some sort indicative of the essential nature of God, and of His wondrous personality. It seems intended to answer in some measure the inevitable enquiries of the human soul, What is God? Does He know, does He care, does He feel? Can He help, can He keep, can He love? If so, will He? The name Jehovah, with the exposition, which God Himself immediately gives of it to His servant Moses, satisfies all these natural cravings of the soul. It blessedly anticipates the long-subsequent expression of that grandest fundamental truth of Inspiration, "God so loved the world!"

Was ever that little word "so" freighted with such a momentous responsibility before?

We will first notice the circumstances under which the name Jehovah was originally communicated. We read in the third chapter that as God was commissioning His servant Moses to go in His name and rescue Israel from Egypt, that Moses very naturally asked, " And when I go to the children of Israel and say, The God of your fathers hath sent me, and they shall say, What is His name? what shall I say unto them? And God said unto Moses, I Am that I Am; and He said thus shalt thou say unto the children of Israel, I Am hath sent me unto you" (Ch. iii. 13, 14) Now assuredly God was not playing with His people, who were at that time in grievous bondage and under cruel sufferings, that He should give them some vague, abstract name, without definite meaning or purpose, or without any hidden blessing, or surprise of grace, or supply of power? It could not be a mere abstract, philosophical name, it must be one full of Divine meaning and delivering grace, pregnant with comfort, and hope, and assurance, such as suffering humanity needs under extremest circumstances. But why was it reiterated and emphasized at this particular juncture? Glance at the fifth chapter for an instant. We find here how disheartened Moses and Aaron were when they came out from Pharaoh, after laying before him God's urgent command to let Israel go and hold a feast unto the Lord in the wilderness. Pharaoh refused indignantly to listen to the request. "Ye are idle, ye are," he said; "you want more work to do. This is but a pretext for idleness; harder work will soon put an end to such spiritual dreams." So he commanded that in future straw should e no longer provided for them as heretofore, but that they should find straw for themselves wherever they could, and yet fulfil the same amount of work. It is indeed an old story of Eastern despotism, still to be seen only too often in Eastern lands, as in Morocco, for example, to this day, though not far from our own shores. This extra hardship sorely afflicted God's people, who were frequently beaten for not doing what was beyond human power to do. So they waylaid Moses and Aaron, and addressed them reproachfully, "The Lord look upon you and judge, because ye have made our savour to be abhorred in the eyes of Pharaoh, and in the eyes of his servants, to put a sword in their hand to slay us" (*v.* 20). As much as to say, the interference of Moses and Aaron had only increased their misery, and the blame rested upon their shoulders. Now we read a significant sentence about the conduct of Moses under this trial. "And Moses returned unto the Lord, and said, Lord, wherefore hast Thou so evil entreated this people? Why is it Thou hast sent me? For since I came to Pharaoh to speak in Thy Name, he hath done evil to this people; neither hast Thou delivered Thy people at all" (*v.* 22). And is it not too often so with us, when God is beginning to work a work of deliverance, that at first things only seem worse than before? Are we not often tempted to say, "I think I shall give up attempting to please God; it only makes me more miserable, for I so constantly fail; it is no use attempting the impossible. Why not live as other people do, and take things easily? Perpetual striving only irritates and worries."

Let us now take special note of what took place between God and His sorely-tried servant. Moses went in at once, and told God exactly what the people had told him. He kept back nothing. He said in effect, "Lord, how is it all this has happened? I did what Thou bidst me to do, and I thought it was for their good; but it is just the reverse. And they blame me for it; and yet really it does not belong to me, Lord, but to Thee." Oh, that we had the same free access to God as Moses had, the same humble but blessed intimacy with the Lord to-day, so that we should instinctively go in at once and lay every trouble, and trial, and reproach at His feet; even expostulating with God, if needs be, when it seems at all justifiable to our poor human judgment, until He shall take us in hand and make us see the matter from His own point of view, and silence all our doubts and questionings. "They went and told Jesus," not that it could be of any use, for the cruel deed was done, and it was too late; but it was of every use to themselves to share their sorrow with their Lord. But how does God answer Moses? "Then the Lord said unto Moses, Now shalt thou see what I will do to Pharaoh: for with a strong hand shall he let them go, and with a strong hand shall he drive them out of his land." This is "what I will do to Pharaoh." God knows how to touch hard hearts, and to turn tyrants to suppliants. And then at once God makes this revelation of Himself, which revelation is the turning-point of the whole story; for do we not find that a deeper vision of God is the true starting-point of personal deliverance with us all?

"And God spake unto Moses, and said unto him, I am the LORD: and I appeared unto Abraham, unto Isaac, and unto Jacob, by the name of God Almighty, but by My name JEHOVAH was I not known to them" (Exod. vi. 2, 3). Commentators are divided as to whether these words are to be taken as a question, "Was I not?" or as an assertion, "I was not"; the latter is more usually adopted.

We will now notice, in the next place, what was contained in the Name thus communicated, or reiterated, at such a crisis in Israel's history. Jehovah itself means the self-existing One, the self-subsisting One, the self-sufficing One, the

All-present, the Eternal Being. And God may be defined to be that One who has the whole of His perfect and unlimited life in His own possession and power, consciously and continuously every moment. In one word, He is Jehovah. Let us then observe carefully how much is involved in this Name, and how thereby the Past, Present, and Future of God are discovered to us, by His own express declaration, to be graciously disposed towards His needy people.

I. *The Completeness of God's Great Redemption* as thus revealed. First, the irrevocable covenant in the *Past*. "And *I have* also established My covenant with them, to give them the land of Canaan, the land of their pilgrimage, wherein they were strangers" (*v.* 4). *I have* established it; it is irrevocable. Second, the Omniscient sympathy, "And *I have* also heard the groaning of the children of Israel. I have heard, Moses, before you told Me; I have heard all." God cannot but hear, such is His Divine nature. Third, "And *I have* remembered My covenant." The unalterable faithfulness of God. These are the three Divine "I haves" of the past, the blessed past of the child of God. We have a God whose covenant is irrevocable, whose sympathy is omniscient, and whose faithfulness is unchangeable.

Now, as to the *Future*, what has Jehovah to say? "Wherefore say unto the children of Israel, I am the Lord, and I will bring you out from under the burdens of the Egyptians" (*v.* 6). This is the first of the seven Divine "*I wills*," which are the inalienable property of the child of God. The future is filled to the full with God's most blessed "I wills." As we travel onward in life, hour after hour, we are only passing from one Divine "I will" to another. "*I will* bring you out from under the burdens; surely this is the identical Gospel message itself, "Come unto Me, all ye that are weary and *heavy laden.*" Whatever it may be, the burden of sin, the burden of trial, the burden of responsibility, "I will bring you out from under the burden." He sees where we are as regards the burden—right under it —" I will bring you *out from under.*" The people under the burden are the people God has got His eye upon; they are nearer to the heart of God than the king upon his throne. This is God-like; this is Jehovah.

But further, " And *I will* rid you out of their bondage, and I will redeem you with a stretched out arm, and with great judgments." First from under the burden of guilt, it must be, then from the bondage of the habits of evil that are keeping you down so that you cannot be free. I will bring you out from under the burden, and forth from the bondage, and I will redeem you, " buy you back " into liberty. " So fetch them home, blessed Lord," is the beautiful expression of our Good Friday collect. " I have seen, I have seen the affliction of My people. I am come down to deliver them!" Liberty means song and thanksgiving. But "how can you sing the Lord's song in a strange land?" The thing is impossible; you cannot do with it there, and yet God cannot do without it.

So you must be brought out first, and when you are brought out, and have come forth clean out of Egypt under the sprinkled blood, and are safe behind the Red Sea, "then sang Moses and the children of Israel"; and woman's voice shall peradventure lead the minstrelsy, as woman was first to fall. For to her came first the gracious rebuke, "Woman, why weepest thou?" and from her sounds forth still in the van of all the Church's praises, "My soul doth magnify the Lord, and my spirit hath rejoiced in God my Saviour." And so to-day, "He hath put a new song in my mouth," whenever the mighty outstretched arm of the Lord is revealed afresh at some recent crisis in each solitary child's history.

And again notice, "And *I will* take you to Me for a people, and I will be to you a God" (*v.* 7). Most blessed "I will" surely. "I will take you to Me." Sweetest of all words! God stays not at rescue from sin and bondage, but "I will take you to Me." No condemnation and no separation! This is our Jehovah Himself as revealed by Himself; and this is the gospel of Jehovah, earlier than any Sinaitic manuscript. He takes the miry bondslave straight from the brick-kilns into His own bosom. Until one day this shall be spoken of as the choicest and most coveted of all distinctions and honours for the redeemed life, "that disciple who leaned on Jesus' breast at supper!" "I will take you unto Me for a people," and the people becomes actually "a peculiar treasure unto Me," a kingdom of priests and a priesthood of kings.

But we have a still fuller "I will" (*v.* 8). Not only will I bring you out, and take you unto Me, but "*I will* bring you *in* unto the land, concerning the which I did swear to give it to Abraham, to Isaac, and to Jacob; and I will give it to you for an heritage: I am the Lord." In short, I will bring you out, I will take you to Myself, I will bring you in! "I will bring you into a land"—it is the land of the oath—how irrevocably ours! It is the land of gift: "I will give it to you for an inheritance"—how irresistibly free! Such is the revelation of the glorious "I wills" of Jehovah, like a vista of the clustered pillars of His shrine, retreating in glittering perspective, strong as Omnipotence, and sun-smitten already with the advancing gospel dawn of His advent.

But it may be asked, Is there no Divine *Present* for the child of Jehovah? Or is the present treated as but an imaginary line between past and future, simply the meeting-place of the two, and almost invisible,—which is indeed just what it is. Where Jehovah's "I haves" and "I wills" meet, there is the standing place of the believer: this is the believer's Present, represented by and over-canopied with Jehovah's great "*I Am.*" For besides the "I have" and "I will," we find "I am" also wrapt up and packed away by the hand of God Himself in this wondrous Name Jehovah. God's renewed promise which we have here unrolled before us, studded with "I have" and "I will," opens with His "I am," like some rich illuminated initial letter in an ancient missal—"*I am* the Lord" (v. 2); and midway we have it again,—"Wherefore say unto the children of Israel, *I am* the Lord" (v. 6); and once more at the close (v. 8),—"*I am* the Lord." It is like some precious covenant or deed, or like some solemn blood-bought international treaty, which is sealed on the first page, and sealed in the middle, and sealed at the end. Just as some wills which require the signature to be on every page for security, so this is the covenant, the everlasting covenant, between the Great Eternal God and the wandering tribes that haunt the borderlands of Time; and the signature of The Eternal must needs be repeated for security on every page. It must be sealed within and without with the great Seal of the Kingdom, "I am the Lord." There can be no change, therefore, here, with the three "I Ams" attached to it. The Trinity have set their seal to it; witness their several signatures: "I am the Lord," "I am the Lord," "I am the Lord." Here is the greatest moral certainty in the universe. Everything on earth or of man changes and shifts and moves, but "I am the Lord" is unchangeable; for though He layeth the beams of His chambers on the variable waters of ministering creatures, this remaineth firm as the very floor of eternity itself. It may seem strange at first sight to some, perhaps, but the man Christ Jesus has the very same motto on His seal as this of Jehovah—"Jesus Christ, the same yesterday, to-day, and for ever."

But how was this Gospel of Jehovah welcomed by Israel? "And Moses spake so unto the children of Israel; but they hearkened not unto Moses for anguish of spirit and for cruel bondage" (*v.* 9). They were so deaf with sufferings and fears, that they could not even hear it; they were so blinded with tears, that they could not catch the golden gleam of hope and sympathy glowing through every word of the Divine message. Is not this the exact counterpart of ourselves to-day?

> "Blind unbelief is sure to err,
> And scan His work in vain;
> God is His own interpreter,
> And He will make it plain."

II. *The Identity of Jesus with Jehovah.*

The completeness of Divine redemption as revealed under the Name Jehovah is now shown in the New Testament to be accomplished in the person of Jesus of Nazareth. In other words, Jesus Christ fulfils all the offices and undertakings of

Jehovah, as regards past, present, and future in connection with His people. Instead of issuing a new copy of the Old Covenant in New Testament times, with renewed demands and penalties, the Covenanter Himself has come, and fulfils His own law in His own person, and discharges all those convicted under it, attaching them at the same time to Himself by personal forgiveness and faith, and covenanting to work out His own life in them, after giving His own death for them.

Who has ever ventured to take up and adopt unto himself the stupendous language of Jehovah which we have been considering,—the "I have," and "I will," and "I am"? None but the Crucified alone.

Calvary says, "I have." "I have made an end of sin."

Resurrection says, "I am." "I am He that liveth, and was dead, and, behold, I am alive for evermore."

Ascension says, "I will." "I will not leave you comfortless; I will come unto you."

Pentecost says, "I do." "I do pour out my Spirit upon all flesh."

"He hath shed forth this which ye do now see and hear." In a word, whereas in the old text, "Thus saith the Lord" rings out on every page, in the Gospels Christ's "But I say unto you" quietly, but significantly, takes its place. Surely He who could say truthfully those three brief words,—"I have," "I will," "I am," in their supreme sense, must be Divine. Who ever ventured before in solemn prayer to Almighty God, and that in the hearing of others too, to recapitulate with perfect approbation all the motives and actions of a lifetime, without one word of confession, or the slightest suggestion of self-accusation or shortcoming?

Let us pause to observe how in that one great prayer alone (John xvii.) there are nine distinct "I haves," in which Christ declares His perfect life-work for His people.

"I have glorified Thee on the earth" (*v.* 4).

"I have finished the work which Thou gavest Me to do" (*v.* 4).

"I have manifested Thy Name" (*v.* 6).

"I have given unto them the words which Thou gavest Me" (*v.* 8).

"I have kept those that Thou gavest Me" (*v.* 12).

"I have sent them into the world" (*v.* 18).

"I have given them Thy glory" (*v.* 22).

"I have known Thee" (*v.* 25).

"I have declared unto them Thy Name" (*v.* 26.)

Surely the Divine ideal life here is complete in all points. And mark what emphasis our blessed Lord lays upon the manifestation of the Name. What Name? Is it not this very Name, Jehovah, which He maintains that He has manifested and declared? Instead of asking, like Moses, what name He should declare, He unhesitatingly asserts His own perfect and intimate knowledge of the Name, and the fulness and faithfulness with which He has communicated it. Here is at last fulfilled,—" I will set Him on high, because He has known My Name." Take again the " I will " of Jehovah. Did ever any son of man venture to adopt this sovereign word of power? The Crucified is that one alone who dares to lay His hand on the leper, and say, " Leper, I will "; and forthwith, by that one word, the leprosy is expelled; and who at the same time dares to lay His hand on the throne, and say, " Father, I will," and therewith admits sinners to glory. Here are nine " I wills " of Jesus Christ, six of them centring round the Ascension :—

" I will ; be thou clean."

" I will come and heal him."

" Father, I will that they whom Thou hast given Me be with Me where I am."

"*I will* pray the Father, and *He shall* ———."

"I will send Him unto you."

"I will come again and receive you unto Myself."

"I will love him."

"I will manifest Myself unto him."

"I will give you rest."

Mark here the perfect command over sin and disease. Mark also His perfect equality with God the Father—"Father, I will"; and His perfect equality with God the Holy Ghost—"I will send Him unto you." Mark also His perfect ability to communicate Himself, and His rest, and His love. And does not this rest which Christ so sublimely promises correspond exactly to the rest Jehovah had promised of old—"I will bring you *out from under* the burdens," "Come unto Me, all ye heavy laden, and I will rest you;" "I will take you *to Me*," "I will receive you to Myself;" "I will bring you *in*," "We which have believed do enter into rest."

But, once more, who but He, the Crucified, has ever dreamed of or dared to take up the challenge of the Eternal God conveyed in the brief but boundless appellation, "I am"? Who but He has ever dared to fill in, and that without hesitation or ostentation, that illimitable blank cheque of Divine potentiality contained in the pregnant title, "I am"? Take again nine examples :—

"Before Abraham was, I am."

"I am the Light of the world."

"I am the Way, the Truth, and the Life."

"I am the Resurrection and the Life."

"I am the Good Shepherd."

"I am the Bread of Life."

"I am the True Vine."

"I am the First, and the Last, and the Living One."

"I am Alpha and Omega, the beginning and the ending, saith the Lord, which is, and which was, and which is to come, the Almighty."

Here He claims to be coeval with Jehovah. He claims to have Life in Himself. He claims to be the Light of the world, the Life of the world, the Food of the world, the Shepherd of the world. He claims omniscient sympathy—"*I am*, be not afraid" (Greek). He claims omnipresent companionship—"*I am* with you always, even unto the end of the world." He claims, as we see in the Revelation, equal eternity with the Triune God, and adopts for His own the very one absolutely unique and literal equivalent to Jehovah, with all its awful mystery and unchangeable indeclinability. In our Lord's own one pregnant word, "Ye believe in God, believe also in Me."

Now let us turn from the I have of Calvary, and the I am of Resurrection, and the I will of Ascension, to the "I do" of Pentecost. "Behold I send the promise of My Father upon you!" "I will do it!" No more words now, but deeds. No more promises now, but prompt fulfilment. Thus affirms Pentecostal Peter—"This is that which was spoken!" Surely everything in the Acts bears witness to the ascended Christ's faithfulness when He said, "That will I do, because I go to My Father."

Wind, and earthquake, and fire, and still small voice, all echo, "This is that which was spoken?" Three thousand converts in a day, all echo, "This is that which was spoken!" "He hath shed forth this which ye now see and hear," echoes again. "This is that which was spoken." Great grace upon all, great boldness, great power, great fear, great joy, all echo the same. Death-stricken Ananias and Sapphira bearing awful witness to the presence of the Lord of life and death, surely repeat the same—"This is that which was spoken!" Stephen's face, aglow with angel light in the council chamber of death, testifies to the same. The miracle of healing at the Beautiful Gate of the temple; Peter's prison doors burst open without hands; "Æneas, Jesus Christ maketh thee whole"—all testify aloud, "I will do it! this is that which was spoken!" Saul converted on the highway, the Ethiopian in the desert, Cornelius the Roman officer in his own house, Lydia by the river side—testify alike, "This is that which was spoken!" Wind and Spirit fulfilling His word! What need we further witness?—"Thou art the King of glory, O Christ!"

Thus have we found that all the actual qualities attributed to Jehovah as regards past, present, and future in the Old Testament are shown to be realized to the full in the person of Jesus Christ in the New. And just as Jehovah was revealed to Israel when they were at their last extremity and compelled to make bricks without straw, so is Jehovah Jesus revealed now to the spiritual Israel, when goaded by conscience to fulfil the righteousness of the law in their own strength, they cry unto the Lord "for anguish of spirit and cruel bondage."

III. *The name Jehovah restored after many days.*

It may well be asked, what has become of the Hebrew name Jehovah in the New Testament. Is it entirely and for ever lost? What! when God gave it at such a momentous crisis, and with such pomp, and with such emphasis? Impossible. But what has become of it? The Jew, indeed, uses it to this hour, he ever prays to Jehovah. Although to him it is so sacred a word that he scarcely dares to pronounce it audibly, habitually lowering his voice with awe, and in reading aloud always substituting the more ordinary name Elohim.

Let us turn to the last book of the Bible, and at the opening of the book (Rev. i. 4) we shall find what has become of the long-lost name. "John to the seven churches which are in Asia: Grace be unto you, and peace, *from Him which is, and which was, and which is to come.*" This is none other than the literal rendering of the grand old Hebrew name Jehovah, which is here restored to us in all its ancient, vast, elemental grandeur and mystery. The glorious name long lost is now recovered to us in Christ Jesus, and recovered to us (glory be to His holy name!) with all redemption's renewed emphasis about it, and with more than all its primal music and majesty. Here is the same unchangeable, self-existent, self-sufficing, grand, abstract, elemental God; yes, but no longer simply abstract and indefinable, the great eternal Essence; for though He is still the Great Spirit, He is also something more: henceforth He is the revealed Triune God from whom grace and peace for ever proceed.

The completeness of Divine redemption is now finally and fully proclaimed before the universe, as proceeding alike and simultaneously from each person of the glorious Triune Deity. Grace and peace being the triumphant outcome and expression of the past, present, and future of the Everlasting and Almighty Lord. " Grace be unto you, and peace, from Him which is, which was, and which is to come ; and from the seven Spirits which are before His throne ; and from Jesus Christ, who is the faithful witness, and the first-begotten from the dead, and the Prince of the kings of the earth."

The Boundless, the Infinite, the Eternal, is here revealed to us as our own great Redeemer-Lord, from whom all fountains of grace and peace are for ever flowing forth. Have we ever stopped and solemnly taken in what is here affirmed? First, that from all the threefold eternity of Godhead, Past, Present, and Future, there is for ever streaming forth grace and peace. Secondly, that from all the sevenfold Holiness of Godhead, here likened to seven lamps of fire burning before the throne, with intolerable light and all-consuming glory, there is for ever streaming forth Grace and Peace. Thirdly, that from all the threefold revelation of

God in the face of Jesus Christ, "whether as "the Faithful Witness" and Prophet of inexorable Truth; or as "the First-begotten of the dead," and the Priest who has returned from His self-immolation on the altar of atonement for the children of death; or as King to whom all power is given, "the Prince of the kings of the earth"; there is for ever streaming forth grace and peace. Grace, the Christ-liberated, all-blessed nature of God—Peace, the Christ-purchased rest both of soul and body.

But not only have we here revealed to us Jehovah expanded into the Three Persons of the Godhead; but still further, and more amazing still, do we find (Rev. i. 8, 17, 18) our blessed Lord claiming to Himself the triple eternity of the Triune God, "I am the first, and the last, and the Living One," as though the Three Persons were all veritably compressed into His own single, glorious Person. And so, as we have said before, we find Him adopting as His very own the one absolutely unique and literal equivalent to Jehovah, with all its magnificent and awful mystery, and all its unchangeable indeclinability (as the nominative case in the original clearly indicates). "I am Alpha and Omega, the beginning and the ending, saith the Lord, which is, and which was, and which is to come, the Almighty!" Shall we not, therefore, here once again, but with deeper awe than ever before, join in the sublime and heaven-inspired doxology to our glorious Jehovah-Jesus?—

"Unto Him that loveth us, and loosed us from our sins by His blood; and He made us to be a kingdom, to be priests unto His God and Father; to Him be the glory and the dominion for ever and ever. Amen. (R.V.)

There are four brief reflections which naturally arise from the consideration of this subject as we conclude. Let us observe, with all thankfulness:—

(1) How the unity and cohesion of Holy

Scripture is mightily confirmed by thus tracing down the ages the wondrous continuity and unbroken development of the name, character, and purpose of Jehovah right onward until the great consummation.

(2) How the sacrifice of the Cross, by the consideration of the absolute and inseparable unity of the Blessed Trinity, is triumphantly vindicated from all cruel and libellous attacks, such as would suggest that God had dealt unrighteously in suffering the innocent Christ to become the sinner's substitute. Whereas we find it to be incontrovertibly true that "God was in Christ reconciling the world unto Himself."

(3) How the grand primal object, expressly contemplated by Jehovah of old, that His people should become a kingdom of priests to offer spiritual sacrifices, has at length been triumphantly attained and manifested in Christ, who "hath made us kings and priests unto God."

(4) How the unlooked for re-appearance of the Song of Moses, in conjunction with that of the Lamb, in the book of Revelation seems henceforth to be invested with a far profounder significance, and to be touched with a diviner illumination, and to breathe an almost indescribable pathos of conflict and triumph, not of this world only.

"Therefore, with angels and archangels, and with all the company of heaven, we laud and magnify Thy glorious NAME, evermore praising Thee, and saying, Holy, Holy, Holy, Lord God of Hosts, heaven and earth are full of Thy glory; glory be to Thee, O Lord most High!"

Cap 2   *JEHOVAH-JIREH; OR THE VICTORY OF DIVINE SELF-SACRIFICE*

"*Behold the Lamb of God that taketh away the sin of the world.*"

"*And Abraham called the name of that place Jehovah-jireh: as it is said to this day, In the mount of the Lord it shall be seen.*"—GEN. xx. 14.

WE come now to Jehovah-Jireh, "the Lord will provide," or "Jehovah will interpose"; and, according to the well-known statement in the Epistle to the Hebrews, "He that cometh to God must believe that He is," first of all; and after that, "that He is a rewarder of them that diligently seek Him"; so in the previous pages we saw that "He is," that He is the self-existent One, the eternal One, and now under this title we shall see that "He is a rewarder of them that diligently seek Him"; and that there can be no question about it.

"In the mount of the Lord it shall be seen."

I. *The walk of faith.*

In the opening verse and onwards we find the walk of faith exemplified in the character and conduct of the great patriarch Abraham. We read in the opening verse,—

"And it came to pass after these things, that God did tempt Abraham"; and yet he was not found wanting. "By faith Abraham, when he was tried, offered up Isaac."

God tempts to prove, to purify, to enrich, and to bless. The devil also tempts; but he tempts to deprive, to despoil, to deteriorate, to destroy; he is the tempter, and then the accuser of the brethren, after being first their seducer and deliberate betrayer.

And when Abraham was thus tried or

God, we read in the same verse, God said unto him,—

"Abraham : and he said, Behold, here I am."

Mark the immediate answer. If you are in touch with God, the answer will be immediate : Here am I. God will always have something to say to you, and do with you, if you are in immediate touch with Him.

"Abraham said, Here am I." Then He said,—

"Take now thy son, thine only son Isaac, whom thou lovest, and get thee into the land of Moriah ; and offer him there for a burnt offering upon one of the mountains which I will tell thee of."

It is a walk of faith indeed,—faith all the way along. He returns an immediate response, and at once prepares for early and immediate action.

"And Abraham rose up early in the morning, and saddled his ass, and took two of his young men with him, and Isaac his son, and clave the wood for the burnt offering, and rose up, and went unto the place of which God had told him."

Immediate obedience; that is the secret of blessing. the secret of peace, and the secret of power.

"And on the third day Abraham lifted up his eyes, and saw the place afar off." The third day is ever the time for resurrection manifestation.

"And Abraham said unto his young men, Abide ye here with the ass; and I and the lad will go yonder and worship, and return unto you again."

Worship! This is the great object and aim of the Christian life. Worship! Not merely on our knees, but in the soul, and in the life; the worship of God's holy will.

Oh! how empty our churches would be if it were only they who have surrendered their wills that entered them. And yet this is the only worship that God recognises,—the worship of a yielded will.

"And we will go yonder and worship." Let the Lord choose the place; anywhere He directs.

Are you willing to worship to-day in this true sense, and anywhere?

"And Abraham took the wood of the burnt offering, and laid it upon Isaac his son; and he took the fire in his hand, and a knife; and they went both of them together."

And then we catch this solemn word from Isaac, the first word he seems to have spoken,—

"And Isaac spake unto Abraham his father, and said, My father: and he said, Here am I, my son. And he said, Behold the fire and the wood; but where is the lamb for a burnt offering?"

And here comes in the sublime answer of the father of the faithful—

"And Abraham said, My son, God will provide Himself a lamb for a burnt offering."

God will provide! Atonement is God's

first and great provision for man's need. All else follows. "Seek *first* the kingdom of God and His righteousness, and all other things shall be added unto you." This is the provision of God made on Calvary. You feel sure ever after that when you are going to give up anything, God will provide. When you have lost everything, God will provide. Jehovah-jireh! This is the walk of faith. Now let us look at the passive side of faith, as represented in the character of Isaac.

II. *The work of faith.*

What is the work of faith? "It is God that worketh in us both to will and to do."

You will observe in the character of Isaac what the work of faith was,—half obedience, and half silence. One of the sublimest things in the world is this character of Isaac,—obedience and silence. He simply obeyed and was silent.

Who was the Isaac of the New Testament?

"Ah!" you say, "the blessed Lord Jesus, undoubtedly."

Yes! perfectly true. He is the supreme Isaac of the New Testament. But there is one other also who seems to me to represent Isaac almost to perfection. Who is that? Lazarus, the brother of Mary and Martha. And this Gospel-Isaac rehearses the death in his own person of Calvary, and goes actually through the figure of death, yea, and all the dread reality of it. And Lazarus, in going through the reality of death, rehearses in his death the coming death of Christ. The death of Christ was thus rehearsed by His most intimate friend Lazarus a week before Christ died. Lazarus died for Jesus, as it were. He died to exemplify what Jesus was about to do, and to prove beforehand how that He who was the resurrection and the life in his case was about to lay down His own life, and to take it again.

Beautiful character, this, of Isaac! No wonder he was very dearly beloved.

"Take now thy son, thine only son Isaac, *whom thou lovest*" (v. 2).

God knew how he loved him. God knows whom we love and how we love. It had reached even to Heaven that Isaac was dearly beloved of Abraham. God knew what a father's heart the father of the faithful had.

Notice not only how beloved Isaac was, but how he loved in return, for obedience is the test of love.

"And Abraham saddled his ass, and took two of his young men with him, and Isaac his son" (v. 3).

There was no question, no hesitation whatever on Isaac's part; no wondering why it was, or what was coming; he was ready to go. "He *took* Isaac." Yes! he was actually so closely in union with his father, so entirely one with him, that Abraham took Isaac just as he took the wood.

That is what God is looking for. Souls whom He can take, and use for Himself, and glorify Himself in them.

O children of God to-day, are we such yielded souls?

And then we have already noticed that at last Isaac speaks. On the third day, it seems, he addressed his father:—" My father, everything is ready for the sacrifice, but there is no lamb."

" My son, God will provide Himself a lamb for a burnt offering." " My son, God will! My son, God will!" That was enough for Isaac.

He was at once satisfied; he acquiesced in the will and word of God perfectly and freely. God could work in him to will and to do of His good pleasure.

We see first that the walk of faith is heroic and prompt; this is faith's active side. And we see here that the work of faith on its passive side is submissive and silent.

After this answer we have an expression

singularly simple but significant: "So they went both of them together."

Observe this touching, yet infinitely grand word, "they went both of them together." We have had it already in the 6th verse. "And they went both of them together"; together, yet alone, each pensively wondering.

What exquisite unity of soul, exquisite identity with the will of God,—"and they went both of them together." "I and My Father are One."

This is what God wants, that we should just go with Him side by side. Enoch walked with God, "and he was not, for God took him."

And now we pass on from this most beautiful instance of surrender, just pausing as we pass to see how Isaac yields himself up in everything. They came to the place that God had told him of:—

"And Abraham built an altar there, and laid the wood in order, and bound Isaac his son." But where now was the lamb? "And bound Isaac his son, and laid him upon the altar upon the wood."

He simply yielded; strong man that he was, he at once yielded to his father; he did not resist the will of God.

Wonderful picture of the Lord who died. "Lo, I come to do Thy will, O God." Anything, Lord, everything that Thou willest! "Shall He not do what He will with His own?" "The cup which My Father hath given Me, shall I not drink it?"

"And Abraham stretched forth his hand and took the knife to slay his son." What! must the Isaac, the divinely given joy of his life, be sacrificed to a sudden blind fanatical impulse of faith? "*By faith* Abraham offered up Isaac." But Isaac was God's own gift; and must faith give back the gift at call to the Giver, and depend upon the inscrutable faithfulness of a Giver who revokes His gift? Was this the struggle here? We know not, we only know the naked majesty of the faith put forth by the father of all the faithful ones.

III. *The reward of faith.*

"In the mount of the Lord it shall be seen." What shall be seen? Let us study this momentous crisis carefully.

(1) *The waiting God* shall be seen in the mount. "The angel of the Lord called unto him, Abraham, Abraham, and he said, Here am I." Just at the precise moment, just at the exact instant, God appears and interposes. The Lord will provide! Marvellous! Every time I read it I am simply amazed at the infinite spirit of sacrifice on the part of both father and son. But still more am I amazed at the unspeakable awfulness of the Divine sacrifice on Calvary, which seems to burn up with its intensity the tragic human story. What unquenchable awe still rests on that height of Moriah, that hill of sacrifice! and shall we not always find the hill of sacrifice to be the hill of Divine interposition, with a waiting God on the

summit? Go up fearlessly, yea, rise early and go; go up and worship, and you shall find God is ever waiting to meet you there. "Therefore doth the Lord wait that He may be gracious!"

(2) Again, "in the mount of the Lord it shall be seen"—what shall be seen? *The sacredness of the surrendered life* shall be seen. "And he said, Lay not thine hand upon the lad, neither do thou anything unto him; for now I know that thou fearest God, seeing thou hast not withheld thy son, thine only son, from Me." Observe the sacredness in God's sight, yea, the absolute sacredness of the surrendered life of God's child. This is a remarkable point. The moment you yield yourself to the Lord you become His entirely. Isaac seems no longer to belong to Abraham, but to God. "Lay not thine hand upon the lad, Abraham; you have given him to Me, and I have received him of you; I accept the sacredness of the trust. Who shall touch the

Lord's anointed? He is the very apple of Mine eye; I, the Lord, do keep it; lest any hurt it, I will keep it night and day. Lay not thine hand upon the lad—thou art Mine, saith the Lord." It reminds us of the woman who brake the alabaster box on His feet; when the disciples grudged the waste—" Let her alone," said the indignant Master; she belongs to Me! God will always interpose on your behalf if you are wholly yielded to Him. You need not be afraid, nor be for ever vindicating yourself, that poor precious self; leave it to God; "I will vindicate, saith the Lord." "Who shall lay anything to the charge of God's elect? It is God that justifieth!"

We know that Isaac's name means " laughter, or joy," for the derisive smile of once dubious incredulity was lost in the sunshine of that happy child. He was the joy of the father's heart, the light of his eyes; yet God calls back the treasure He Himself had given. The Divine promise was lodged in him alone; yet he must now give up the promise into the hands of the Promiser, he must resign the gracious gift to the Source of all grace, and exchange Divine faith for Divine faithfulness. Instead of for ever poring over our own faith, a far too common sort of introspection, let us dwell deeper on His own guaranteed faithfulness. Observe, O ye believing fathers and mothers, what a splendid offering it was, and how much Jehovah thought of it: "Now I know that thou fearest, seeing thou hast not withheld thy dearest." This is the victory that overcometh the world of sense and sight, even our faith. This is the secret of all want of success in the spiritual life,—we withhold from God, and force Him to withhold from us. "Give, and it shall be given unto you, good measure and running over shall God give into your bosoms!" Withhold the son, or withhold the sin, and you force God to withhold the peace and the power.

Keep back part of the price, and you shut out all the shining of the Presence, and the luxury of the love of the Unseen. Spare the darling sin, and you lacerate your own soul.

"In the mount of the Lord it shall be seen." What shall be seen? The great principle of substitution shall be seen.

(3) *The glorious substitution by Divine provision*, whether it be the ram of Moriah or the Lamb of Calvary, or Jesus for Barabbas. "And Abraham lifted up his eyes, and looked, and behold, behind him a ram caught in a thicket by his horns: and Abraham went and took the ram, and offered him up in the stead of his son."

How healing is this blessed doctrine of substitution to the soul that can offer nothing! Troubled soul, there is nothing to offer; "the Lord will provide; my son, God will provide Himself a lamb for a burnt offering!" God's son in the stead of man's son! The Son of the

Father in the stead of Barabbas, "a son of a father!" Did Barabbas repent as he gazed on his Substitute impaled in his stead? Why was there no John Baptist at the foot of the Cross proclaiming at the sixth hour—"Behold the Lamb of God, that taketh away the sin of the world"? The Egyptian darkness that followed would have been Nature's awful commentary. But you say substitution is such an unnatural doctrine. It is just the reverse; it is a part of the common law of nature everywhere. Nearly every creature is ready to sacrifice itself for its young by a universal instinct. In the hedgerow the parent bird defends with herself her menaced fledgeling; in the cornfield the skylark, to shelter its brood, attracts attention to itself. The mighty mother-instinct of substitution prevails in hedgerow and furrow, in field and forest, and in every human home; why not upon the throne of the Eternal? Commerce is made possible by this inevitable law: the mariner and the miner risk their lives for others' welfare; the soldier's glory is to die for his fatherland. Shall God alone be denied the glory of self-sacrifice, the nobility of substitution? Nay, in the midst of the Throne behold there is "a Lamb as it had been slain!"

"O Saviour, grudging Thee the bitter bliss
Of all men's woe, men rob Thee of Thy Cross—
That landing place of love for shipwrecked souls,
That shore whence God launched forth alone with
    sin,
And plunged it in the deep of His own blood!"

"And Abraham lifted up his eyes and looked, and behold, behind him a ram caught in a thicket by his horns." This is God's unexpected provision on the dark mountain top.

(4) "In the mount of the Lord it shall be seen." What shall be seen? *The reckoning of faith.*

"Accounting, or reckoning, that God was able to raise him up even from the dead; from whence also He received him in a figure." "In the mount" of Calvary reckon yourself to have died verily with Christ for your sins; this is to appropriate the atonement by faith. Resurrection life is the receiving of yourself back again from the dead in a figure. So that "it is no longer I that live, but Christ that liveth in me"; this is to be no figure, but a daily Divine experience. "The one true way to lose self is to love"—"I live no longer unto myself, but unto Him that loved me, and gave Himself for me." This blessed substitution is at the basis of everything we see. Conversion is the appropriation by faith of the Substitute for sin. Resurrection life is the appropriation by faith of the Substitute for self. Consecrated service is the appropriation by faith of the Holy Spirit as the Substitute for self-effort. "I laboured more abundantly than they all, yet not I, but *the grace of God that was with me.*" It is God the Holy Ghost "who worketh in you both to will and to do."

The true believer's life consists in thus saying, "Yet not I," three times—in salvation, in sanctification, in service.

It is on Calvary we see One caught in the dark, tangled thicket of thorny human sins and human sorrows, fast bound to the altar of the cross, torn and bleeding, yet held there by the two irresistible cords of intense devotion to God and man; and as we gaze upon Him, there imprisoned of His own free will, we hear Him exclaim: "No man taketh it from Me; I lay down My life of Myself," and we cannot but repeat with awe from one to another: "Behold the Lamb of God, that taketh away the sin of the world! My son, my brother, God has indeed provided Himself a Lamb!" Jehovah-Jireh! In the mount of the Lord it *is* seen! "And Abraham called the name of that place Jehovah-Jireh." What, the very place of sacrifice becomes the meeting-place with God, the workshop of the Almighty, a platform extemporized for Jehovah's wonder-works; the place where the Lord demands is the place where the Lord provides; "as it is said to this day, in the mount of the Lord it shall be seen." Yes, as it is said to *this day*; Calvary is still the theme in men's mouths. The world cannot stop talking about it, though they tremble at it. Philosophers and infidels, whilst they are repudiating it, are writing volumes about it; they cannot forget it. They date their letters from it, and deny it on the same sheet. The saints love it, and cling to it; they live on it, and live by it; they die for it, and they die on it. The sinner steeped in sin, and drunk with the Circean cup of revelry and shame, calls for it as the one cooling draught of life and peace, which, if he do but taste with dying lips, shall heal the fatal poison in his veins, and let him die in hope. Yes, as it is said unto *this* day, "In the mount of the Lord it *is* seen." Behold the Lamb, always Behold! for you cannot

DIVINE SELF-SACRIFICE

see it except by faith. You cannot believe it; it is too incredible, save as you gaze upon it with the eye of faith.

(5) "In the mount of the Lord it shall be seen." What shall be seen? Something more, *the vision of the Second Voice.* "And the Angel of the Lord called unto Abraham out of heaven the second time" (*v.* 15). This is the second voice so many of us miss. We hear the call to sacrifice, we are forced to hear it, and we reluctantly attend; but we are mostly too impatient to wait for the second voice, the voice of blessing which follows that of demand and sacrifice. How many of us have been in darkest straits and deepest depths of sorrow and suffering and yet have never heard, never listened to hear, the Second Voice. We never knew or recognised that the Lord was calling to us out of heaven the second time. How emphatically it is written, "And the Angel of the Lord called unto Abraham out of heaven the

second time." "Yea, *twice have I heard the same*, that power belongeth unto God." So saith the Psalmist of old, and that which he heard of God's power twice is precisely what we are always needing to hear. The call to sacrifice we hear, but the call to blessing behind it we fail to hear. Oh, for faith behind the brimming tear! Oh, for faith to hear behind the message of God's inevitable will the footsteps of His mercy hastening to our side! " Behind a frowning providence He hides a smiling face," said one who knew what he was saying, and of Whom he was speaking. How sweetly the second call falls on ears full of sounds of sacrifice and awe. How many thousands and ten thousands of Christians have found release through atonement from the terrors of judgment, but have never waited to receive the sweet promises of grace and purity and power! How many thousands, having got by dint of prayer, as they believe, all they need to keep body and soul together, hurry away from the throne and the golden sceptre outstretched to them, never dreaming of "the royal bounty" their King is longing to bestow. Satisfied to be saved and caring for nothing more—is not this the condition of half the Christian Church?" Oh, for hunger for the Second Voice, and its glorious vision!

(6) "In the mount of the Lord it shall be seen." What shall be seen? *The irresistible claim upon God of full surrender.* "By Myself have I sworn, saith the Lord; for. because thou hast done this thing, and hast not withheld thy son, thine only son from Me, that in blessing I will bless thee." Thou hast not withheld, therefore I cannot withhold; such is the Divine principle of action between God and His own children. Presume upon My goodness and generosity, and with contrite prayer you can ask what you will, and it shall be done unto you. Because thou hast not

grudged Me anything I asked, I will give thee all without asking. Such is the irresistible effect of full surrender upon the great Jehovah. First it was, "now I know that thou fearest God, because thou hast not withheld thine only son"; now it is, not only do I know about thee, but thou shalt know about Me, that I am able and longing to do exceeding abundantly above all ye ask or think! O happy repetition of Divine words, but O glorious addition, O blessed indulgence of Divine love! Thou hast not withheld, I cannot restrain!—until at last the child has indeed caught the spirit of the Father: "the love of Christ constraineth me to keep back nothing,—yea, let Him take all, for My Beloved is Mine, and I am His!"

(7) "In the mount of the Lord it shall be seen." What shall be seen? *The outburst of Divine blessing.* "In blessing I will bless thee, and in multiplying I will multiply thy seed as the stars

of the heaven, and as the sand which is upon the seashore; and thy seed shall possess the gate of his enemies; and in thy seed shall all the nations of the earth be blessed; because thou hast obeyed My voice" (*v.* 17-18). What an outburst of blessing! Mark the reiterated "I wills"—I will bless thee, I will multiply thee. Mark the reiterated "shalls"—thy seed shall, all nations shall.

Plenty, power, perpetuity, these are the guaranteed blessings to a fully surrendered soul. Plenty and fruitfulness; not a family, but a firmament, of starlike souls, shall be thine! Power over the enemy, yea, power over all the power of the enemy, shall be thine! Perpetuity, behold, I will bless thee, and thou shalt be a blessing. Thy children shall rise up and call thee blessed; they that turn many to righteousness shall shine as the stars, and in the midst of their own firmament of stars, for ever and ever!

And now why all this blessed unrestrained Divine extravagance of love, we may well ask. Why? "Because thou hast obeyed My voice." Is that really all? Let us read it over again—"because thou hast obeyed My voice." O blessed path of obedience! O Divine recompence of surrender! See what the Divine crucible yields at last, the cruel, burning crucible that seemed to consume all! The mountain of sacrifice is the mountain of supply. Springs of blessing break out on Moriah's mountain-top. A single step—and Calvary turns into Pentecost; the place of bereavement or cutting off is the place of enduement or putting on! The place of every thought brought into captivity is the place of fullest emancipation and boundless possession! The place of the fire and the knife is the place of a sweeter, tenderer knowledge of God, and of deeper draughts of the fountain of life!

"In the mount of the Lord it shall be seen." The tabernacle was according to the pattern shown in the mount. And was not Calvary according to the pattern shown in the mount? And is not Pentecost, too, according to the pattern shown in the mount? Is not, I say, death in solitude the source of life before the world?

IV. *The Rest of Faith.* "So Abraham returned unto his young men, and they rose up and went together to Beersheba; and Abraham dwelt at Beersheba" (*v.* 19). What a contrast the return journey was to the going forth! What a contrast between "they went both of them together," with its infinite pathos, and this "they rose up and went together to Beersheba"! After the visions and the voices and the sacrifice, it is well indeed to make our home by the Well of the Oath. What a place of rest and revival to dwell in, by the Well of the Oath!

This should be the address of every believer, the Well of the Oath. After you have climbed the Hill of Consecration, and yielded yourself afresh to the

Lord, and He has discovered to you the secrets of the kingdom, go straightway and dwell contentedly by the Well of the Oath. The spring of blessing is assured and inexhaustible as the Lord Himself who is yours, and who shall be in you "a well of water springing up unto everlasting life." But what does Beersheba, this Well of the Oath," represent to us to-day? The Well of the Oath is none other than the Well of the Everlasting Word, that Word that liveth and abideth for ever. Therefore with joy let us draw water out of the wells of salvation !

> " Thus all anointed souls are crowned
> By kneeling first, and being bound
> By altar of the Lamb once slain
> In fetters fetterless to reign."

Cap 3 — JEHOVAH-ROPHI OR THE VICTORY OF DIVINE ASSIMILATION

"*I am crucified with Christ.*"—GAL. ii. 20.

"*For I am the Lord that healeth thee.*" Or as it is in the Hebrew—Jehovah-Rophi.—EXOD. xv. 26.

WE have already contemplated the great name of Jehovah in its first elemental grandeur; and then we dwelt upon the Divine sympathy of Jehovah-Jireh, who manifests Himself as a God who interposes and who provides.

We now advance still further, and are taught this lesson, that God is Jehovah-Rophi, "I am the Lord that healeth thee."

What a blessed word to be revealed to the fallen race! What a blessed relationship between the thrice holy God and

His poor erring creatures! "I am the Lord that healeth thee!"

You must have observed in the history of Israel being brought out of Egypt a growth in the principles of spiritual life.

First we have this principle brought out, as the blood was sprinkled on the doorposts in Egypt according to the commandment of God: "When I see the blood I will pass over it." *God sees* the blood of atonement, and it is enough.

And then we come to a further point.

When they reached the Red Sea, the commandment went forth: "Stand still, and see the salvation of the Lord." *Israel now sees.* Believe that God sees, comes first; and then, Israel shall see, comes next. "Stand still, and see the salvation of the Lord."

And now in this chapter, immediately after the crossing of the Red Sea, immediately after a very short journey in the wilderness, we are brought to this further stage, *believe to see.*

DIVINE ASSIMILATION

First, as to the Blood of Atonement, we are to believe that God sees, and to rest upon that.

Then, when it comes, the Church must see to the resurrection lite and the way right through the Red Sea.

And, thirdly, there is this further great lesson forced upon us who belong to the Israel of God.

Believe to see! If difficulties arise, believe to see. If trials come, believe to see. If bitterness occur, believe to see.

You must also have observed, surely, that in this wonderful passage describing Israel's journey out of Egypt through the wilderness, there are three characters that arrest our attention.

First, there is the character of God Himself, the great Jehovah, boundless in compassion, and infinite in resources, so that however often God and His people seem to be driven into a corner, there is always a way out, always some means of escape.

Secondly: we cannot but all have noticed, surely, how that Israel is an example of the up and down life of many in the Christian Church to-day; that though they are ever under God's protection, ever under His mercy, yet that they are for ever murmuring, and for ever rebelling against Him.

Then there is a third life presented to us alongside of these two. Whose is that life? It is the life of Moses.

Marvellous life! A life sustained, inspired, devoted, and undaunted. A man who was unmistakeably a man, and yet who was in constant and lowly communion with God. A man who, though he belonged to Israel and was a pure Israelite, yet lived above the up and down life of Israel, because he lived in constant, unbroken communion with his God. Moses had six hundred thousand people upon him, no light task indeed; and yet only once was he hasty and impetuous, though for that once he was debarred from entering the promised land.

Perhaps in all Holy Scripture there is not such another human character.

You must have noticed also, that after salvation through the blood of atonement sprinkled on the doorposts, and after the crossing of the Red Sea, which indicated the separation of God's people unto Himself; after, I say, the salvation, and the separation, then there followed the song —the song of triumph, led by Miriam, as we read in this chapter,—

"Sing ye to the Lord, for He hath triumphed gloriously; the horse and his rider hath He thrown into the sea."

And now, immediately following the triumph, comes the bitterness of disappointment. That is where we are now (23rd verse)—

"So Moses brought Israel from the Red Sea; and they went out into the wilderness of Shur: and they went three days in the wilderness, and found no water."

I. *The Curse.*—" And when they came to Marah, they could not drink of the waters of Marah, for they were bitter: therefore the name of it was called Marah." Is this, then, all they have got by the three days' march in the wilderness which God demanded from Pharaoh?

Notice, in passing, how this very name Marah is continually associated with the Lord Jesus. Mary is the very same word, Mary was the mother of Jesus; bitterness brings forth sweetness and deliverance. Mary, too, was that very one out of whom the Lord cast the seven devils, rescuing her from the power of evil; Marys, we find, are continually about Him, from the cradle to the cross.

And so we read in the 23rd verse,—

" And when they came to Marah, they could not drink of the waters of Marah, for they were bitter; therefore the name of it was called Marah."

Observe, then, that as soon as we have entered into and realized salvation, and separation, and the song of triumph, then come the suffering and the testing at Marah. We meet the curse and its consequences everywhere. As soon as a Christian is redeemed, and he knows it; as soon as he is separated, and he means it; as soon as his lips are unsealed, and he sings the thanksgiving song of the Lamb; then he is tried, he is proved, he is tested; Marah comes, and he meets the curse. The bitterness of every spring upon earth is the result of the curse, the fall of man and the sorrow which followed it; everything that spoils this fair world is the result of the curse; the curse is the result of the fall, and the fall is the result of man's own sin. We are responsible for all the sadness, and sorrow, and sin. It is a beautiful world in itself, but oh! how marred, how spoiled, how contaminated! As soon, then, as we are thus in reality saved, separated, and brimming over with the song of thanksgiving and triumph, we are brought, as God's Church, not only to face the curse, but to undo the curse wherever we go. Henceforth it is ours to change disappointment into success, bitterness into sweetness; this is the great duty and privilege of the Christian Church; and henceforth, whether we approve of the methods of foreign missions or not, we are bound to approve of this—that all savagery, and ignorance, and sin, and barbarism at home or abroad shall be arrested by every means in our power. You have been saved, you are one of God's own children, and triumph in that wonderful victory of the Lamb, then you must immediately begin at your door, or, it may be, go forth afar, and undo the curse as far as in you lies, turning everywhere some spring of bitterness into a spring of sweetness and joy.

Now we pass on, and we read in the following verse,—

"And the people murmured against

Moses." They were always murmuring This is the beginning of it. When Moses tried to help them, they murmured, and they go on with it right through the wilderness. We can all murmur, I suppose, if we cannot do anything else. But God would teach us here how to be delivered from murmuring.

"And they murmured against Moses, saying, What shall we drink?"

And so it was that he cried unto the Lord, and thus we come to the cure.

II. *The Cure.* — Now that we have glanced at the curse for a moment, we will look at the cure. The cure is of two parts.

The first part is prayer. "And he cried unto the Lord."

Think of the six hundred thousand people murmuring against their solitary leader, their devoted, dauntless leader. "What shall we drink?" Moses, it is all your fault that we have nothing to drink. "And he cried unto the Lord." What a power there is in prayer! What a power in just going at once to the Lord! "He cried unto the Lord." And the answer is immediate and explicit. Read the other portion of the cure:

"And the Lord shewed him a tree, which, when he had cast into the waters, the waters were made sweet." That tree was a type of the Bitter Tree of Calvary.

This is the other portion of it: "The Lord shewed him a tree." It comes to this, that when we are brought to Marah, into difficulty, and trial, and pain, it is a blessed opportunity for God to discover to us some new secret of the kingdom.

What will not a great artist do to become great in his art? What a life of drudgery he lives for it! What does not a great man of science bear? He endures years and years of scorn often, and reproach upon reproach. But at last he finds the secret. "I have found it! I have found it! The secret is discovered!" and it is worth all.

So it is with the child of God. When

he comes to his Marah, his place of trial, the Lord is waiting to discover to him some secret of the kingdom, some divine secret, which shall in answer to his prayer enable him by grace to change the bitter into sweet.

The Jews think that this was a bitter tree itself which changed the bitterness into sweet, on the principle of like healing like. What does it represent to us? To the Christian it represents this, *the Cross of Christ infused into the daily life :* " I am crucified with Christ "! God's recipe for one under a thorn in the flesh, or any other kind of suffering, or in face of any obstacle or oppression, or anything that brings us very low and to our knees, is, " My grace is sufficient for thee." This is the Divine secret, "My grace is sufficient for thee." That is the wood cast into the spring of bitterness, that is the secret of God by which we shall overcome. What a blessed power there is in thus following the example of the apostle, " I will glory in my infirmities." A thorn in the flesh is just a single splinter of the cross left in us to remind us that we *are* crucified with Christ.

We have been complaining of feeling our circumstances utterly insurmountable, "My grace is sufficient for thee." I will glory henceforth in my infirmities, that the power of Christ may descend or rest upon me.

Nay! this wonderful wood of the tree shows us this also, that in cases of sorrow and bereavement, in cases of depression and darkness, God has a wonderful elixir, a marvellous tincture, a few drops of which can turn bitterness into sweetness. That tincture is the will of God. So it was with those in the Acts of the Apostles, of whom we read that when they could not prevail in dissuading Paul from going to Rome and facing all the dangers of martyrdom, they ceased, and said, "The will of the Lord be done."

What a power it was, as we have already seen in the case of St. Paul—"The will of the Lord be done." He could even rejoice in the thorn in the flesh. It was not taken away, but he at length could glory in it. So it was with the blessed Master in the garden of Gethsemane: "Not My will, but Thine be done," He cried. "The cup which My Father hath given Me, shall I not drink it?"

What a change! A few drops of this Divine tincture changes everything, and the very sorrow we feel at this moment, and the bereavement, and the pain, and the separation, can all be healed to-day by a few drops of the cordial of His divine will. Take but as thine own the will of God, that pure and perfect will of God, and it is enough.

But also this wood shows us something still further.

We have not only thorns in the flesh, we have not only sorrows and bereavements, but we have something still deeper.

we have perpetually to meet the disease of sin. What can be done? It impregnates the life, it mars the speech, it causes us to yield to temptation; everything is ruined by this deadly influence, this fatal infection. What shall stop it? Prayer and the Cross. Bitter fountains of temper or tongue, of pride or passion, all may be cured by the cross of Jesus cast into the impure spring of human nature. The root of bitterness may be neutralised by the blessed "Root out of a dry ground," if only applied in faith and honesty. The healing tree was there waiting beside the waters of death. With the preaching of the Cross of atonement there must be also the preaching of *the Cross of assimilation*, that is, co-crucifixion with Christ.

"For the preaching of the Cross of Christ is to the Jew a stumbling-block, and to the Greek foolishness; but to us who are saved it is the power of God unto salvation" from sin as well as from its penalties.

Marvellous deliverance! The Cross of Christ is that which changes the bitterness of this world of sin into the sweetness of Gospel peace and joy, purity and power. The Cross of Christ becomes assimilated with the life.

But I must pass on. And we immediately come upon, in the same verse, the way to ensure this perpetual sweetness in life.

III. *The conditional Covenant* between God and us is read over to us, as it were, by the well of bitterness.

"If thou wilt diligently hearken to the voice of the Lord thy God, and wilt do that which is right in His sight, and wilt give ear to His commandments, and keep all His statutes, I will put none of these diseases upon thee, which I brought upon the Egyptians: for I am the Lord that healeth thee."

The covenant is conditional: that is the next thing to be remembered. It is a conditional covenant,—"If thou wilt

.. I will ... because I am." God distinctly tells them what He expects of them, and then what they may expect of Him. It is a Divine compact. The promise is definitely expressed on God's part' the warning is as definitely conveyed on the other hand, or rebellious Israel shall fare as rebellious Egypt.

It is a solemn thing, this conditional covenant revealed by the spring of Marah. How often it has been repeated in our own case since!

Beloved, if you find that you are not submitting to God's conditions, you had better look to it; you are at the spring of Marah over again; see to it that you do your part in the conditional covenant; hearken to His voice, keep His will and commandment, and then the Lord will deliver you according to His word.

We know what to expect, then, of God, that He will bless us, and keep us, and preserve us, if we keep close to Him. We know what to expect also if we do not—difficulty, sickness, and trial. And remember, moreover, that at the same place where the Lord has made with us the new covenant—the conditional covenant—He at the same time has also given a new revelation of Himself.

IV. *The new Revelation.*

He reveals Himself in some new light. First we saw Him as Jehovah, the self-existent One, who is all-sufficient. Then, secondly, as Jehovah-Jireh, the Lord who will provide and interpose. Now He is, thirdly, Jehovah-Rophi, I am the Lord that healeth thee. It is a new revelation of the Lord.

And there are many souls, I trust, who have thus been brought through deep waters, and who have known what it is to have a new revelation of the Lord by the spring of Marah, where the Lord has revealed Himself under a new name, a deeper and more intimate name,—" I am the Lord that healeth *thee.*" The bitter fountain God here declares to be ourselves.—He seems to address us individually, "O man, O thou human spring of bitterness, I made thee to be a fountain of life-giving water; but, alas! the water is corrupt, the fountain-head is poisoned."

The blessed Lord Jesus finds us hopelessly tainted. His name in Greek is exactly rendered by the English "Healer." That is His true name, Jesus, the Healer,— "I am the Lord that healeth thee!" And so when we come to read His history in the Gospels, we find His three years of public ministry were just a three years' course of practical healing both of soul and body. "I will come and heal him." "He went about healing all those that were oppressed of the devil." How literally true, "He sent forth His Word and healed them."

Notice, then, that we have revealed in this very name just this—that each one of us is a spring of bitterness, which, unless the Healer shall change, will be saltless. Oh, how many people are springs of bitterness in their homes, in their families,—a spring of bitterness always bubbling up! "I am the Lord that healeth thee." You can be healed, temper, passion, pride, envy, and all—"I am the Lord that healeth *thee*." Thou art a spring of bitterness, a root of bitterness, I am come to heal thee!

Oh, how blessed is such a discovery! yea, it is blessed to discover our own bitterness itself; for if so, the Lord will put forth His power and show us that— " I am the Lord that healeth thee."

I ask you, beloved, will you not spend a part of this very day in gaining such self-knowledge, until you cry out for this Divine transmutation for yourself. Will you not go straight to God and say, "Lord, if Thou art the Lord that healeth, heal me, heal me, I entreat Thee, to-day." Moses is a case in point. He healed Moses. Moses was once so passionate that he smote an Egyptian, because he thought it was to the glory of God. As to the healing of the body, St. James has clearly laid down the place of believing prayer in all matters of healing, its unique place and power. At Marah, manifestly, means were used. But God can dispense with means if He sees fit, as at Cana's miracle. His will is supreme here as elsewhere. Thus the fiery Moses soon afterwards became the meekest man upon earth—"I am the Lord that healeth thee."

Doubtless we all are passionate when anything really touches us keenly; unhappily it is no monopoly of any man's, though some men do take the monopoly of it to themselves. "I am the Lord that healeth thee."

We are all failures in some direction or other;. but, "I am the Lord that healeth thee." He will heal us now if we permit Him.

I must pass on, and close.

V. *The coming Compensation.*

We now come to the blessed compensation, the astonishing and abounding compensation of grace (*v.* 27).

"And they came to Elim, where there were twelve wells of water, and threescore and ten palm trees: and they encamped there by the waters."

First of all we read, after passing through the Red Sea, they spent three days in the wilderness, and had no water; and, when they had found water, it was bitter water. How strange it seems! But now, when they have triumphed over disappointment by the grace of the Lord, they come not only to sweet water, but they come to Elim, where there were twelve wells of water—a well a tribe. Thus they passed from no water to bitter water, and from bitter water to abundance of water.

This is God's way of gradual compensation. Oh! strive on, child of God; hold on, beloved, in the Name of the Lord; conquer in His power; and, through His blessed Spirit, do not give way; quit you like men,—

> "Nor bate one jot of hope or heart,"
> But steer right onward,"

as the poet Milton says of his blindness.

Then go down to Elim where there are twelve wells of water—water abounding, life abounding: "I am come that ye might have life, and have it more abundantly."

There you shall find also a blessed screen of shade and tender shelter in the Lord's near Presence overshadowing you and yours. The twelve wells of Elim, and three score and ten—seventy—palm trees, represented, it may be, the Apostles and those who went forth for the Master's work; the seventy disciples, as well as the seventy elders with Moses in the Mount.

"And they encamped there by the waters." Surely it was a good place. I propose that we encamp there to-day in the same blessed spirit of unity with the brethren,—by Elim, where there are twelve wells of water and the seventy palm

DIVINE ASSIMILATION

trees, and that we rest under the shade with hearty thanksgiving and gratitude. Let us eat and drink there the provided meal, eat and drink to be strengthened for the journey of life, for the work of the Lord, "for the journey is too great for thee." Here is the Divine way to encamp:

"I sat down"—a deliberate act at a given time—"under His shadow with great delight"—a definite experience of conscious communion,—"and His fruit was sweet to my taste"—a delicious satisfaction is realized in the perfect will of God.

Christians Divided into Seven Classes.

THERE are seven classes of Christians in the professing Christian Church. And these represent seven stages of belief not unfrequently realized in the experience of many. It will be profitable to consider briefly these various kinds of Christians, and their various classes, so that we may examine ourselves, and ascertain to which class we belong, and still further ascertain, if possible, how we may advance from one class into the other.

First of all there are :—

(1) *Nazareth Christians,* if I may so call them

These are they who believe in Christ as a perfect example of humanity, the solitary flower of the whole human race; though at the same time they freely deny His divinity, and discard His claims to the supernatural; they repudiate and discount His teaching, as too often being affected by ignorance or personal bias or ambition; and yet in the midst of all this they look upon Him as the ideal One, the solitary human Exemplar, the world's one moral mirror, they attempt to follow Him as far as may be, and uphold His character in a measure, and defend Him in their own various ways.

And yet this blessed Lord Jesus, whom they look upon as the ideal Man merely, was for ever arrogating to Himself every attribute conceivable of Godhead; He was for ever declaring of Himself that He was, and He only, the source, spring, and fountain of Divine law and all other truth :

" For this cause was I born, and to

this end came I into the world, that I should bear witness to the truth."

And yet, in spite of this, your Nazareth Christian discards half His teaching as mythical, and uttered under the influence of personal feeling or patriotic ambition.

This is the first class of Christians, if we may call them such.

The second class are of a very different stamp.

(2) *Calvary Christians.*

These go a whole stage further. The first class of so-called Christians believe in Christ as the Example and Teacher, though at the same time they declare that His example is imperfect, and His teaching is not wholly to be trusted.

Calvary Christians are they who believe in the pardon and peace which God gives through the atonement on the Cross of Calvary.

They are Christians who are exceedingly careful to be clear that the blood of Jesus Christ has blotted out all their transgressions. They believe that through the offering of Jesus Christ on the cross they need not die eternally, they need not suffer the penalty of sin, because it has been endured in the person of Jesus as their Substitute.

They hold, therefore, that God hath already granted to those that believe pardon, free pardon; and that which follows immediately out of pardon—peace, perfect peace, through the blood of Jesus Christ.

Oh! blessed are these Calvary Christians who thus know what it is to have sin blotted out and sin forgiven, and who now "go in peace," as the blessed Master Himself has commanded them to do.

You may ask, How may we pass from being a Nazareth Christian to a Calvary Christian? Let me put it in one word. Fasten your whole attention upon the problem of sin, and its absolute irremediableness, save through a Saviour from above. And if you have any real moral power or perception, you will be bound to pass from the first stage of believing in the ideal Christ to believing in a Christ who is indeed the ideal Man and Exemplar, but who died that He might raise His followers to His own moral position, and free them from the curse of sin, and from the penalties of God's holy law.

There is a third class. These are

(3) *Easter Christians*, or Resurrection Christians.

They go further. They believe, indeed, that Christ is the ideal Man; they believe, indeed, that in His offering on the Cross there is complete pardon and peace. But they go further, and they believe that He is also risen—risen from the dead to be an assurance to His people of deliverance from all fear, bondage, impotence, failure, and defeat.

Easter Christians! Would that they were more plentiful.

So many Christians are quite content to stay at the cross, and if they can only believe that the blood of Jesus hath cleansed them from sin, and that through that precious offering of the Lord Jesus they may enter into peace, they are satisfied.

But those who are honest in thus believing are bound to go forward, because they feel that they in themselves are weakness, failure, and uncertainty; that there is a constant precariousness in their faith and walk, therefore they need indeed to become Easter Christians, so to call them; that is, to have the full assurance of the risen Saviour, and to realize the life of deliverance which is offered so freely through the resurrection of Jesus Christ.

"All power is given unto Me in heaven and in earth."

But there is yet a further class of Christians, for I pass rapidly on; and this following class of Christians is a very large class. It is composed of what I may be allowed to call

(4) *Forty-days' Christians.*—Before our

blessed Lord went home to heaven forty days elapsed. Forty-days' Christians belong to this transition period.

Doubtless you have observed that during the forty days when our risen Master was upon earth He used to appear constantly to His followers, and then almost immediately disappear again. He would mysteriously appear where He was obviously absent a moment before, and then He would disappear again. When the disciples were assembled within closed doors, suddenly, without any visible entrance, Christ appeared in their very midst.

I would describe these forty-days' Christians as Christians who know, and know only, the up-and-down Christian experience.

There is intermittency as to the presence of Christ, as far as these are concerned. He comes and He goes. One time they are full of joy; just as of old: "Then were the disciples glad when they saw the Lord." But at other times they are deeply depressed, they are full of sorrow and apprehension; they need to be encouraged, and assured whether they are Christians or not; they want some fresh confirmation that they are Christ's and Christ's wholly, and they want to be assured that Christ is theirs, and always theirs.

This is what I call a forty-days' Christian—one who has this fitful experience, this intermittent experience of the Presence, and the joy, and the glow of the Lord Jesus Christ.

How many there are who know only this experience! How many there are who, if they honestly spoke the truth, would have to say, " That is precisely my own experience. At times I am full of assurance, full of peace, and comfort; at times it is the greatest joy to serve Jesus, I would give up anything for Jesus."

Of course, that is only a form of speech. It means generally that you give up as little as possible; but we frequently use this phrase, "I would give up anything for Jesus; I am so full of His presence and His strength, because He is with me;" and then to-morrow we are all full of faults and failures: apprehensive, if but a passing cloud is over the house, that it will be always dark, that God has forgotten to be gracious, and has actually given them up.

It is like that simple Roman Catholic woman, who exclaimed when her crucifix was broken, "Now I have nothing but Almighty God to trust in."

But besides this these Forty-days' Christians have also this characteristic—there is a want of cohesion between them and others. You must have noticed, if you have read carefully the account of the forty days, what a kind of breaking up there was between all the disciples; how they fell apart at once like a rope of sand—distracted and bewildered, one goes this way and another goes the other. There was no cohesiveness among them, if I may use the expression; there was a great want of central attraction, and consequently of mutual cohesion. There was necessarily also an entire absence of all unity of action, and, of course, of aggressiveness of any kind. These are the chief characteristics of the Forty-days' Christian. First, there is a want of cohesion through the presence of Christ being intermittent. Secondly, there is an unaggressiveness in his experience, because he cannot be sure of himself or others.

That is the secret of the charge so often brought against so many Christians to-day, that they have so little union or unity. They are only Forty-days' Christians; there is no aggressiveness, because there is an entire absence of cohesion; and this is the case because the presence of the central power of attraction is fitful, and they are not sure that Christ is theirs and that they are Christ's. Intermittency, want of cohesion, want of aggressiveness—these are the ancient and unfailing marks of the Forty-days' Christian.

But there is yet a further class that immediately follows upon this—

(5) *Ascension Christians.*

They are those who go still further. They have, by God's grace, arrived at this point—they have perceived that there is a blessed cohesion among the Churches of Christ because they realize communion with their ascended Lord, and freedom of access into the eternal Presence, even upon the throne!

Ascension Christians are those of whom it may truly be said that "their conversation is in heaven"; that they do in some true and real degree "dwell in heavenly places"; that they find such an attraction in Jesus as to raise them above this world and to lift them heavenward; the opened heavens giving them a glimpse, as it were, of the transfiguration mount, and a holy intimacy with the Unseen World.

This gives them that upliftedness above the world which often confounds and disappoints ordinary Christians who go to them to talk the ordinary world talk; their friends fail to respond with the heartiness that worldly people do, because the heart is really engaged and pre-occupied with heavenly things, and, as our Prayer-Book so beautifully puts it, they have "in heart and mind thither ascended, and with Him continually dwell."

But there is a further class, as, of course, you perceive at once, there is a further class yet, for there are seven classes of Christians, and this further class consists of—

(6) *Pentecost Christians.*

A Pentecost Christian is a Christian who possesses Christ and is possessed by Christ, and is in the conscious occupation of God the Holy Ghost, and who is thereby filled with a great desire and yearning to bring in others to the feet of Jesus. That is a true Pentecost

Christian. It is one who is cleansed and inspired by the Holy Ghost; it is one who, being himself possessed by the Spirit of God, pursues after others to bring them in also to the feet of Jesus Christ. Possessed and pursuing, these are the marks of the Pentecost Christian—Spirit-possessed and soul-pursuing.

I have only one word further to add. There is yet the seventh class. What more can there possibly be, you say?

We have glanced at the Nazareth Christian, the Calvary Christian, the Easter Christian, the Forty-days' Christian, the Ascension Christian, and the Pentecost Christian; what further class can there be? There is one more stage yet, marked, emphatic, all-important.

(7) *Advent Christians.*

The Second Coming of Christ, the return of Christ for His own people, and His entrance upon His own blessed eternal kingdom,—this is the mightiest spiritual incentive of all.

Advent Christians: these, if they be real Advent Christians, include all others. These are they who perceive that with His return there will be a great gathering in of souls; these are they who perceive that the Coming of Christ is that which shall make the whole difference to all God's vast creation; these are they who perceive that the whole earth is travailing in pain, and that it is waiting for the adoption, to wit, the manifestation of the sons of God at the Coming of Jesus Christ.

But you say, if you fasten your attention on the return of Jesus Christ you will forget your work. Not at all. Because the true Advent Christian perceives that it is only by hastening on the work that he can hasten on the Return of Jesus Christ and His kingdom. Representatives from every part of Redemption's Kingdom must be present on Coronation Day.

Shall we not at once interrogate our

own hearts in the conscious Presence of God? To what class do I belong? Be not content, but go on, I beseech you, unto perfection; go on until you reach the blessed highest class, the Advent class, which includes all other classes, and be prepared, as He has commanded us to be, with loins girded and lamps burning, to meet your Lord when He returns for the bridal of His Church.

But how are we to pass from one class to the next? By discovering carefully, and fastening your attention upon the weak point in the experience of each class or stage. And then you will soon discover the divinely appointed provision set over against it. Thus under the keen pressure of your own defective and dissatisfied experience, stirred by your deep soul-disappointment, you will search the Word till you find the Key to deliverance, and the passport to the next stage. The Nazareth Christian, fixing his attention upon the insoluble problem of sin, and how it remains altogether unrecognised by his class, can never rest till he become a Calvary Christian. And a Calvary Christian, recognising the bondage and weakness of his daily life-experience, can never rest till he become an Easter Christian. And an Easter Christian, though he enjoy resurrection liberty, perceives the absence of the companionship of the Presence, and in spite of himself he becomes a Forty-days' Christian. And the Forty-days' Christian, disappointed with the intermittency of fellowship, reaches forward to the sustained and steady vision of an Ascension Christian. And the Ascension Christian, discerning the danger of selfishness in the joy of Divine communion unshared, learns to exchange his own solitary bliss of communion for the God-like generosity of communication, which distinguishes the Pentecost Christian. And the Pentecost Christian, stimulated by the joy of Divine communion and of the still diviner joy of communication, is caught up unawares, as it were, and kindled with the anticipation of the glory of the manifested Person of the King, and of the consummation of His growing kingdom, till, inspired and thrilled by a divine impatience, he becomes an Advent Christian, waiting, and working, and wrestling to hasten the coming and coronation of the Saviour-King and Lord.

THE
SPIRITUAL GRASP OF THE EPISTLES;
OR,
AN EPISTLE A-SUNDAY.

By Rev. CHARLES A. FOX, B.A.,
Incumbent of Eaton Chapel, Eaton Square.

Second Edition, now ready.

MARSHALL BROTHERS,
KESWICK HOUSE, PATERNOSTER ROW.

www.ingramcontent.com/pod-product-compliance
Lightning Source LLC
Chambersburg PA
CBHW030406170426
43202CB00010B/1506